Original title:
Petal Puns and Other Fun

Copyright © 2025 Creative Arts Management OÜ
All rights reserved.

Author: Juliette Kensington
ISBN HARDBACK: 978-1-80566-608-0
ISBN PAPERBACK: 978-1-80566-893-0

## Folly of the Foliage

Leaves giggle in the breeze,
Whispering sweet mysteries,
Branches sway with silly grace,
Dancing all over the place.

Laughing at the buzzing bee,
Who can't seem to find his tea,
Nature's jesters all around,
In this folly, joy is found.

## **Droll Dandelions**

Dandelions make a wish,
With every puff, a funny dish,
They scatter seed, a playful jest,
A grassy joke, at nature's best.

Laughter in a sunny field,
Bright yellow armor, they won't yield,
Tickling toes of passersby,
These cheeky blooms still reach for the sky.

## Amusements of the Aloe

Aloe's spines like funny hair,
They sprout up in wild affair,
With a grin, they soak up sun,
In their world, we'll always run.

Chilling out, they laugh and glow,
In every pot, a show must go,
Silly faces that they make,
With every wink, a giggle's break.

## **Cheery Cherries**

Cherries dangling, oh so bright,
Winking down with pure delight,
They gossip sweetly all day long,
In their orchard, all is strong.

Join their merry, vibrant cheer,
Each juicy bite brings laughter near,
With playful pits that tease and laugh,
A cherry dance on nature's path.

## Merry Marigolds

In the garden, golds dance bright,
Tickling bees till the fall of night.
Laughing leaves in the sun's embrace,
Join in the jolly, a floral race.

With every bloom, a joke unfolds,
Petal giggles in marigold molds.
Nature's jesters, in colors bold,
Whisper secrets that never grow old.

## Capering Carnations

Whirling pinks with a cheeky grin,
Twirl to the tunes when the sun is in.
Dancing stems on a breezy day,
Making the bumblebees stop and sway.

With every blossom, a laugh they share,
Carnations caper, here and there.
A sprinkle of humor in every hue,
Their fragrant giggles, a joy anew.

## **Verdant Vignettes**

Leaves spin stories in shades of green,
Whispering tales of the unseen.
Giggling grass under skipping feet,
Frolicking ferns, oh what a treat!

Nature's canvas, a playful scene,
Woven whims, like a jester's dream.
In every curl, a chuckle does bloom,
A funny little world only flowers consume.

## The Whimsical Weeds

Oh, the weeds with their sly little smiles,
Making mischief in their own wiles.
Rambunctious sprouts in the garden's heart,
Crafting chaos, a cheeky art.

They laugh and dance in wild parade,
While the careful blooms feel dismayed.
With every tug, they pop up with glee,
A hearty chuckle, wild and free.

**Grinning Geraniums**

In the garden, laughter grows,
Geraniums giggle, with rosy shows.
They sway and dance in the sunny rays,
Winking at bees in silly displays.

With petals bright, they tease the breeze,
Spreading joy like honey with ease.
Each bloom a joke, a punchline too,
Cheering up all who've come to view.

## Lively Leafy Laughs

Leaves are chuckling, green and bright,
Whispering secrets in morning light.
They tickle the branches, quip and sigh,
As butterflies giggle and flit nearby.

A rustle here, a giggle there,
Nature's jokes hang in the air.
Every leaf a little jest,
In the forest's funny fest.

## Chortles in the Chrysanthemum

Chrysanthemums chuckle, both bold and proud,
Their vibrant hues shout out loud.
They jostle and jive in a flowery wiggle,
As squirrels below stop to giggle.

A daisy slips, with a flirty grin,
As runners buzz with laughter within.
In this floral bash, no room for frowns,
Just joy and cheer in flowery gowns.

## **Floral Frolics**

In fields of blooms, where humor reigns,
Flowers compete in silly chains.
Daisies reveal their topsy-turvy,
While violets dance, feeling so swirly.

Roses crack wise, with thorns in jest,
Making sure they give guests a quest.
Amid the petals, laughter spreads,
A frolic of colors, where fun never ends.

## Jovial Junipers

In a garden where giggles grow,
Junipers prance in a breezy show,
They sway with shoes painted bright,
Dancing away the morning light.

With branches that tickle the sun's warm face,
They whisper jokes that set the pace,
"Why did the shrub just unite?"
"To leaf behind worries, take flight!"

Their laughter sound like rustling leaves,
Crafting humor like spiders weave,
"Let's vine together, let's be a pair,"
"Let's root for each other, show we care!"

So wander where these junipers play,
And join in their jests, laugh away,
For nature's comedy is the best,
With jovial tones, leave out the rest.

## The Laughing Lily Pad

On a pond where giggles drift and glide,
Lily pads parade with a buoyant pride,
They wear little hats, perched so balanced,
As frogs croak puns with ribbits of talent.

"Why can't flowers ever break the rules?"
"They might get caught handing out drool!"
With every splash, a chuckle can rise,
Fish chiming in with sparkling eyes.

A rabbit hops by with a wiggly ear,
"Why did the lily feel no fear?"
"It knew how to float and make people cheer,"
As laughter echoes, soft and clear.

In this scene of humor, joy's a must,
The pond's a stage, a laugh-filled crust,
So come join the splashy, giggly parade,
Where puns bloom bright, and cares fade.

**Happy Hydrangeas**

Hydrangeas giggle in the breeze,
Dancing wildly with such ease.
They whisper jokes that bloom and grow,
In vibrant hues, they steal the show.

With petals round and colors bright,
They tickle our hearts, a pure delight.
Each laugh they share, a splash of glee,
A garden carnival, can't you see?

## **Eloquent Eucalyptus**

Eucalyptus trees stand tall and proud,
With branches swaying, they draw a crowd.
They tell tall tales with fragrant air,
And make us chuckle without a care.

Their leaves are green like vibrant dreams,
Whispering secrets, or so it seems.
Meanwhile, koalas munch away,
Laughing at life, come what may!

## **Jesters of the Jungle**

In the jungle, jesters leap,
With playful roars that make us peep.
Monkeys swing and drums they beat,
Their antics make our hearts skip a beat.

Parrots squawk with vibrant flair,
Spreading humor everywhere.
With every twist, they set the tone,
Life in the wild, a laugh-filled zone.

## Babbling Blossoms

Babbling blossoms share a tale,
With colors bold that never pale.
They giggle up with morning dew,
A garden chat that feels brand new.

Their petals wave like little hands,
Inviting us to join their bands.
In every bloom, a secret hides,
A world where laughter never slides.

## Vine Vibes

In the garden of laughter, I find my glee,
The flowers are chuckling, can you hear their spree?
The daisies dance lightly, they've got such flair,
While the roses are blushing, with tales to share.

The sunflowers wink as they stretch all day,
They nod their heads gently, come what may.
The ivy whispers secrets, a mischievous tease,
As nature's own humor brings us all to knees.

## Sprout Smirks

Little sprouts giggle, peeking from the ground,
With tiny green jokes that are quite profound.
They poke fun at the weeds that try to invade,
"Oh look, here comes trouble, a lawn renegade!"

With each droplet of dew, they sparkle and shine,
The garden's comedians, their timing divine.
As mushrooms break into giggles, round and stout,
They chant, 'We're fun-guys, no need to pout!'

## **Nature's Nitty-Gritty**

In the thicket of humor, the critters unite,
With a squirrel's quick quip that brings pure delight.
The frolicking rabbits, with leaps full of glee,
Say, "Have you heard? We've got tricks up our sleeve!"

The brook babbles softly, with water's sweet rhyme,
As the dragonflies dance, keeping perfect time.
Nature's own jesters, they playfully tease,
Chasing each other with the softest of breeze.

## Jokes in the Jungle

In the jungle so lush, where the wild things play,
The monkeys are laughing at the games they display.
With vines as their swing sets, they climb with such cheer,

Saying, "Swing by for puns, we're always here!"

The parrots squawk jokes with the brightest of flair,
While sloths just hang out, with napping to spare.
The jungle's a circus, with quirks around,
Nature's own comedy show, so profound!

## **Smirking Succulents**

In the garden, greens conspire,
Cacti joke in the sun so dire.
With spines that tickle, they laugh aloud,
Sipping water, feeling so proud.

Aloe winks with a soothing glow,
While little orbs put on a show.
Whispering secrets, they twist and twirl,
These smirking succulents love to unfurl.

## Cheerful Cheerios

In a bowl where smiles reside,
Cheerios dance, they can't hide.
Round and golden, they roll about,
Bouncing with laughter, no room for doubt.

Milk splashes, a bubbly cheer,
As O's play hopscotch, loud and clear.
Dropping jokes, they're quite a scene,
In breakfast bowls, they're living the dream.

## Witty Willows

Willows sway with a clever twist,
Branches quip in a gentle mist.
Rustling leaves share giggly glee,
Telling tales of a buzzing bee.

With every bend, their humor grows,
Jokes on the wind, everyone knows.
In every shadow, laughter's found,
Witty willows, a comic crown.

## **Jocular Junipers**

Junipers grin with berry cheer,
Spreading joy, oh so near.
With prickly jokes that poke and tease,
They make the sun shine with such ease.

Bending low, they share a jest,
Nudging each other, they're truly blessed.
In fragrant whispers, they sing and tease,
Jocular junipers sway in the breeze.

## Chuckling Clovers

In a field where green clovers play,
They giggle and sway, come what may.
A four-leaf finds luck, so it claims,
While three leaves just chuckle at names.

A jester plant, with a wink and a spin,
Sprinkles its humor as the day begins.
Each leaf a laugh, each stem a tease,
In their leafy kingdom, time bends with ease.

## Gleeful Gladiolus

Gladiolus stands tall with flair,
Its colorful blooms catch the air.
With a wink and a nod, it does prance,
At the garden ball, it leads the dance.

Flowers shout, "Let's make a scene!"
As the gladiolus grins, bright and keen.
With petals like laughter, bold and bright,
It fills the garden with pure delight.

## **Playful Petunias**

Petunias burst forth in shades of fun,
Each bloom a joke, each color a pun.
They twirl in the breeze, spinning tales,
With scents that dance and never fails.

Whispers of joy float on the breeze,
As petals tease bees with silly pleas.
In their patch, laughter is the theme,
Where blooms weave wonders, like a dream.

## The Joyful Juniper Journey

Junipers chuckle, a merry bunch,
Rolling along, seeking their lunch.
With berries that giggle at every turn,
And needles that shimmer as they yearn.

Through forests lush and hills so wide,
They sing of adventures, full of pride.
With every step, they bounce and sway,
On this joyful journey, they find their way.

## Witty Wildflowers

In the garden where jokes take root,
Daisies dance in their snazzy suit.
Roses share tales from their thorny past,
While tulips giggle, their futures forecast.

Buttercups boast of their sunny delight,
Chortling softly in the cool moonlight.
The daisies tease with a playful cheer,
Creating laughter all around, oh dear!

Lavender sways, spreading scents divine,
As marigolds mutter, 'We're simply divine!'
Petunias wink with their colors so bold,
The garden, a stage where tales unfold.

A daffodil's pun leaves others in stitches,
While sunflowers sway like comedic witches.
Blooming with humor from root to the tip,
In this wildflower world, we all lose our grip!

**Cherished Chortles**

In fields of laughter, jokes take flight,
Tulips sharing giggles, what a sight!
With every bloom, a chuckle grows,
Sprouting quips like laughter flows.

Forget-me-nots giggle, 'We won't fade away!'
While lily pads joke at the end of the day.
Silly sunflowers bask in the fun,
Claiming their rays leave no one outdone.

Petunias chuckle, their petals all bright,
Spreading joy beneath the moonlight.
Courageous cosmos dare to be loud,
Their comedic stances making them proud.

In this garden of cheer, joy takes a spin,
Every flower knows how to grin.
Together they bloom, brightening our sights,
In a tapestry woven of pure delight!

## Whispers in the Flora

Whispers flutter in the gentle breeze,
As violets hum tunes that aim to please.
Foxgloves gossip with their bell-shaped charms,
Sharing inside jokes of leafy farms.

Petals plot mischief, oh what a scene,
What will happen when the garden is green?
A daisy jokes, 'I'm just here for the fun!'
While the becalmed orchids melt in the sun.

A rose teases white with a colorful jest,
'You're all very pretty, but I like to fest!'
As zinnias dance, twirling with glee,
The floras share secrets, oh what a spree!

In every shadow, each nook and nook,
Petal tales echo, so come take a look.
With roots that delight and leaves that sing,
The garden holds joy in everything!

## **Blooming Laughter**

In a patch where giggles sprout with grace,
Every blossom wears a smile on its face.
The daisies chime in, a chorus so sweet,
Joking with joy, they can't be beat.

Sunshine tickles the blooms on high,
While peonies wave, piercing the sky.
With every breeze, laughter takes wing,
In the garden of humor, they burst and sing.

The fussy orchids whisper with pride,
'Being this fabulous can't be denied!'
Chrysanthemums chuckle, their heads held high,
Joking with bees as they flit and fly.

With petals a-flutter, the pranks never cease,
In this vibrant world, we find our peace.
For in laughter's bloom, hearts never tire,
In this garden of joy, we all conspire!

## Zinnias and Zingers

In a garden bright and spry,
Zinnias wink and say hi.
With colors that make you grin,
They tease the bees—'Let's begin!'

One zinnia danced with flair,
Said, 'I'm too cute to be rare!'
The sunflowers rolled their eyes,
'Just don't get lost in your size!'

'You think you're such a star!'
Crooned the daisies from afar.
'With your roots all tangled, dear,
We're pretty sure you're a mere cheer!'

But zinnias just wink and twirl,
'Let's add some fun to this whirl!'
With laughter that fills the space,
They spread joy with every trace.

## Fuchsia Frolics

Fuchsia flowers bounce and sway,
Insisting on a bright ballet.
'Look at us, we're so divine!'
They prance around the garden line.

With petals waving like a fist,
'Better watch out, don't you miss!'
Their frolics lead to giggles loud,
A flamboyant, blooming crowd.

One fuchsia claimed, 'I'm the best!'
While others chirped, 'We're all blessed!'
They danced till dusk, spun through the air,
A show of petals beyond compare.

Underneath the moonlight glow,
Fuchsias steal the garden show.
With every twirl and every spin,
They remind us—let the fun begin!

## Marigold Merriment

Marigolds bask in the sun,
Cheerful rays that make them run.
With golden faces bright and bold,
They laugh at tales of ages old.

'Why are we always so bright?'
They giggle, what a delight!
They whisper jokes to passing bees,
'You buzz around just to please!'

A marigold with petals wide,
Said, 'I'm the sun's favorite ride!'
While others echoed with hearty cheer,
'We bring the warmth all through the year!'

In gardens filled with joy's embrace,
Marigolds thrive with endless grace.
With laughter echoing through the day,
They paint the world in a joyful way.

## Petal Poetry

In a meadow of sweet delight,
Flowers whisper, taking flight.
'Let's pen some verses, shall we try?'
Petals fluttering, oh my, oh my!

A rose begins with verses slick,
'Roses are red, but here's the trick!'
The daisies chuckle, 'We'll join the fun,
With laughter that weighs a ton!'

They write of sunshine, warm and bright,
Of buzzing friends that take to flight.
Their rhymes are silly, bold, and true,
Mixing joy in every hue.

So gather 'round, let's start the show,
With petals dancing in a row.
In gardens where the giggles bloom,
Petal poetry sweeps the gloom.

## Snapdragon Snapshots

In a garden filled with cheer,
Snapdragons snap, oh dear!
Watch them grin and jaw they play,
As they chat the day away.

Snap at me, I'll bite right back,
With a joke, we'll hit the track.
Giggles echo, laughter swells,
In this land of floral spells.

**Blooming Banters**

Daisies dance with glee and wink,
Spreading joy with every blink.
They giggle, twist, and turn around,
In a game where cheer is found.

Roses tease with their sharp wit,
Blooming jokes, they just won't quit.
Petals flutter, laughter flies,
In a realm where humor lies.

## Aster Antics

Asters prance with flair and style,
Witty puns that make you smile.
They toss their leaves and twirl about,
In a playful, lively shout.

With every bloom, a laugh erupts,
Nature's jesters, fun and chucks.
Jokes that blossom, laughter shared,
In this garden, all are bared.

## **Zinnia Zeal**

Zinnias cheer with colors bright,
Spreading joy from left to right.
With quick quips, they light the day,
In their quirky, playful way.

Each flower beams with vibrant looks,
Telling stories, casting hooks.
Join the splash of colors bold,
In the laughter that unfolds.

## Frivolous Ferns

Frolicking ferns in shady glades,
Dance with whispers, a joy parade.
They chuckle softly in leafy disguise,
Nature's jesters, oh, how they surprise!

Beneath the sun, they sway and shake,
With each gust, they giggle and quake.
They tease the breeze, a vibrant fling,
In laughter's grasp, their green hearts sing.

With a wiggle here and a twirl over there,
Ferns share their joy without a care.
Sprouting jokes from deep in the dirt,
Nature's humor, bright and alert!

So if you see them, join their game,
Twirling and laughing, it's never the same.
For frivolous ferns in their playful way,
Bring fun to the garden, come out and play!

**Laughter in Lavender**

Lavender blooms with a fragrant jest,
Spreading smiles, they know how to dress.
Tickled by bees in a vibrant glow,
They whisper secrets as soft winds blow.

In fields of purple, they sway and tease,
Bringing mischief with every breeze.
With scents of cheer that shimmer and sway,
They tickle noses in a jovial way.

Booked for humor, they never disappoint,
Each petal a punchline, a fragrant joint.
With laughter brewing in lilac delight,
They giggle softly, day into night.

So join the jest in lavender's finery,
Where giggles bloom in blushing irony.
In the garden of glee, let your worries subside,
With laughter in lavender, come take a ride!

## Punny Petunias

Punny petunias in pastel hues,
Sprout silly smiles with witty cues.
They whisper quips in a floral style,
Each blossom bursting with humor and guile.

Their petals flutter like jokes on the vine,
Sprinkling laughter, a twist so divine.
With each blooming joke that's fresh and keen,
They paint the day in the brightest sheen.

Gardeners grin at their colorful tease,
Punny petunias put spirits at ease.
With a chuckle here and a snicker there,
Their playful fun floats in the air.

So join the laughter, take a little chance,
With punny petunias, let's twirl and dance.
Their garden giggles are hard to resist,
A bouquet of joy, you won't want to miss!

## Mirthful Meadows

Mirthful meadows where daisies play,
Giggle and wiggle through bright, sunny days.
With a swirl of colors, they frolic so free,
Sprouting joy in a raucous spree.

Butterflies flutter with laughter and glee,
Joining the chorus of blooms in a spree.
Each petal's a giggle, a bounce of delight,
In meadows of mirth, everything feels bright.

Fields filled with joy, where the sun paints the sky,
Nature's own laughter floats gently by.
In the dance of the flowers, we find that we're kin,
Mirthful meadows, let the fun begin!

So skip through the fields, let out a laugh,
Join in the fun on nature's own path.
For in every blossom and buzz all around,
Mirthful meadows share joy to be found!

## Rosebud Revelry

In the garden, roses grin,
With each bloom, a cheeky spin.
They whisper jokes in fragrant tones,
While bees buzz loud on weathered cones.

With petals soft, they make a tease,
Puns like nectar, sweet as bees.
In merry blooms, they dance and sway,
Bringing laughter to the day.

Thorns may poke, but laughter's near,
With every rose, a hearty cheer.
They twirl in bright and rosy hues,
Sharing secrets, laughing too.

When the sun smiles, the petals wave,
In the breeze, their jokes they save.
In rosy jest, they celebrate,
A blooming joy that's truly great.

## Daffodil Drollery

Daffodils, with golden glee,
Tell tall tales of bumblebee.
In sunny patches, laughter rings,
As they waltz and stretch their wings.

Their petals prance, a silly crew,
With jokes that tickle, always new.
They nod their heads in springtime fun,
Chasing down the warming sun.

In fields so bright, the giggles fly,
With every breeze, they shimmer high.
Daffodils, in yellow's hold,
Share stories funny, bold, and gold.

When morning breaks, they catch the light,
With laughter loud, a cheerful sight.
In every bloom, a chuckle blooms,
A joyful splash, dispelling glooms.

## Colorful Quips

In the patch where colors blend,
Quips and giggles never end.
Violets wink and daisies smile,
Making every moment worthwhile.

Zinnias shout their cheeky puns,
While warming in the afternoon sun.
Petunias join with tales so bright,
Creating laughter, pure delight.

In hues so rich, their jests are bold,
Rainbow blooms, a sight to behold.
With every breeze, they share their mirth,
A garden full of jolly worth.

With petals wide and laughter free,
The world grows light with their spree.
Colorful quips that lift the soul,
In nature's joy, we all feel whole.

## Pollen Pranks

The pollen flies in cheeky whirl,
As flowers giggle and twirl.
Sunflowers give a sunny wink,
With every breeze, they start to think.

A lilac's laugh can shake the ground,
With each new joke, joy is found.
In every bloom, a twist or two,
Spreading humor as they grew.

The tulips lead with silly tricks,
While daisies join in funny flicks.
With every petal, laughter spreads,
In floral jest, joy is fed.

With nature's fun, the day ignites,
Pollen pranks bring pure delights.
In fragrant blooms, the smiles reside,
A garden party, laughter wide.

**Blossoms in Jest**

In the garden, blooms do tease,
With whispers carried by the breeze.
Roses roll their eyes with flair,
While daisies giggle without a care.

Tulips tell tales of a sly bee,
Whose dance was just too clumsy, you see.
Sunsets blush from laughter all night,
As flowers chuckle in moonlight's light.

Carnations poke fun at the weeds,
For their tangled tricks and stubborn deeds.
With every joke, they spread their grin,
In the garden, where laughs begin.

So come and join the merry scene,
Where petals play like a festive screen.
In blooms of laughter, we take a rest,
In this garden, we are truly blessed.

## **Laughing Lilies**

Lilies dance in a gentle breeze,
While chuckling softly at buzzing bees.
"Hey there, friend, don't take a dive!"
"Stay on the petals, come on, thrive!"

Daffodils prance, oh what a sight,
Waving their heads in pure delight.
"Why did the stem? It couldn't leaf!"
"Oh, please don't tell that to the chief!"

In every bloom, a joke unfolds,
Under the sunlight, where laughter holds.
They give a wink and share a laugh,
Creating joy on nature's path.

So when you wander through this space,
Join the flowers in their silly race.
For in their world, there's endless glee,
With giggles shared by you and me.

## Sunflower Shenanigans

Sunflowers grin, tall and proud,
With heads that turn and laugh aloud.
"Do you see that cloud over there?"
"Looks like a fluff with naught to spare!"

Their seeds trade stories of sunny days,
Giggling round in twisting ways.
"Why did the flower cross the street?"
"To get to the sunshine, it's hard to beat!"

In fields of gold, a festival grows,
With tricks and flips that everyone knows.
"Hey butterfly, do a spin!"
And soon the dance begins to win.

Laughter rides the warm summer air,
As petals burst with joy to share.
Join the sunflowers, don't be shy,
In this blooming joy, we all fly high!

**Saved by the Stem**

With roots in the ground, so sturdy and strong,
The plants share a tale that can't be wrong.
"Why did the cactus bring a friend?"
"To help with the hugs—it's a prickly trend!"

A daisy laughed at the gardener's scheme,
"Caught with the weeds? Oh, what a dream!"
Tulips chimed in with their vibrant chorus,
"Let's throw a party, don't you adore us?"

The ferns waltz on the cool, green turf,
Witty remarks added to the mirth.
"Knock, knock! Who's there?" a blossom proclaimed,
"Lettuce in—the party's not the same!"

In this patch, where green meets delight,
They gather to giggle and celebrate light.
With every stem, laughter grows wide,
In this botanical world, come and join the ride!

## Chuckles in the Canopy

In leafy halls, the laughter grows,
Silly squirrels strike a pose.
A parrot's joke, a bird's punchline,
Even daisies whisper, 'We're divine!'

The branches shake with giggles bright,
Breezes howl with pure delight.
A rabbit grins with carrot glee,
Says, 'I'm the funniest one you'll see!'

The sunbeam's rays dance through the trees,
Painting smiles on playful leaves.
With every rustle, a jest is spun,
Can you catch the punchline? Just have fun!

So while you roam beneath this sky,
Remember laughter's never shy.
Join the bloom, get in the game,
In comedy's garden, all is the same!

## **Flora in Frivolity**

A flower's joke blooms on the vine,
'I'm just here for the punchline!'
Bumblebees buzz with buzzing wit,
Quick as a wink, they never quit.

Even cacti wear a grin,
'Prickly humor's where I begin!'
Roses laugh, their thorns aside,
'Take our humor in your stride!'

Underneath the joyful sun,
Nature knows how to have fun.
With every bud that starts to grow,
Comedic spirit starts to flow.

In fields of color, jokes take flight,
Laughter blooms both day and night.
Let every petal play its role,
As laughter's beauty fills the soul!

## **Giggles Among the Greens**

Among the greens, a chuckle plays,
'What's a tree's favorite holiday?'
The answer's given with a wink,
'Tree-mendous fun, don't you think?'

Olive branches sway with glee,
'We're too cool, just wait and see!'
As painted petals dance with grace,
Laughter matches their embrace.

A leaf drops down, it tells a tale,
'I've traveled far, I won't fail!'
With every twist, a pun's revealed,
In every shrub, a joke concealed.

So wander deep through this green land,
With humor and joy, take a stand.
Gather giggles along the way,
Nature's laughter brightens the day!

## The Comical Cosmos

Stars twinkle like they have a joke,
While moonlight glimmers, shadows poke.
'Why did the planet feel so blue?'
'Cause it had no rings to dance in too!'

The comet zooms with a bright, bold flair,
'Catch me if you can, if you dare!'
Galaxies swirl in playful spins,
'This cosmic dance is where it begins!'

Asteroids hum a merry tune,
While space is filled with laughter's boon.
In the void, the quips take flight,
With every flicker, pure delight.

So gaze above and let it show,
That even stars love to glow.
In this vast, uncharted space,
Laughter finds its perfect place!

## **Blossom Whispers**

In the garden where sunflowers grin,
Bee buzzes dance, and daffodils spin.
Petals gossip, in colors so bright,
Sharing secrets from morning till night.

Lilies wear laughter like a bright crown,
Spreading good vibes all over the town.
Tulips play tag with the warm summer breeze,
Chasing the bees, oh, such silly tease!

Rose bushes chuckle in rosy delights,
While daisies join in, taking flight.
Nature's own jesters, so lively and free,
Winking at frogs perched on a leafy spree.

Every bud beams with a joke of its own,
In a world where cheerfulness has grown.
Let's join the giggles, let's join the cheer,
In our floral haven, there's nothing to fear.

## Tulip Tickles

Tulips are ticklish, oh what a scene,
Giggling soft whispers, all around green.
With petals that flutter in rhythm and rhyme,
They dance to the beat of the passing time.

Dandelions blow wishes up high in the air,
While pansies wink back without a care.
Every flower giggles when compliments bloom,
A tickle of laughter can lighten the gloom.

Fleeting and playful, these blooms bring cheer,
Their jokes are so fresh, it's clear they're sincere.
Humor in gardens, where joy blooms anew,
A secret shared among petals so true.

So if you feel down, just stroll through this patch,
Where flowers conspire to bring you a laugh.
With every bright petal, they'll lift you today,
Tulips will tickle your troubles away.

## Daffodil Delights

Daffodils dance with a sunny delight,
Winking and nodding from morning till night.
They chuckle in clusters, so golden and bright,
Making hearts flutter, oh what a sight!

A rose once remarked, 'What a stylish move!'
While violets whispered, 'Let's all join the groove!'
With laughter that rolls like a soft summer breeze,
These vibrant blooms sway with effortless ease.

Grinning marigolds share their tales of cheer,
Swinging their leaves as the butterflies steer.
Ticklish blooms giggle with each gentle sway,
Creating a riot of color and play.

Let the daffodils brighten up your day,
In the garden of humor, we'll all sway.
Join in the laughter, the mirth on display,
For joy's just a bloom away, come what may!

## **Blooming Laughter**

In a field of giggles, where blooms spread wide,
Every petal shines with humor inside.
Buttercups crack jokes, oh what a sight,
As bees roll in laughter, in pure delight.

Chrysanthemums chuckle with colors so bold,
Whispering secrets that never grow old.
With every sweet breeze comes a comedic twist,
Flowers unite, for a laughter-filled bliss.

Jasmine joins in, with a whimsical sway,
Sharing sweet stories on a sunny bouquet.
The garden is bursting with smiles to share,
Where even the thorns join in without care.

So come take a stroll through this laughter parade,
With blooms full of puns that never do fade.
In the laughter of flowers, there's joy to be found,
A symphony of fun on floral ground.

## Orchid Odes

In a pot of soil, I dance with glee,
Too many blooms? Quite the spree!
With colors bright and scents to share,
I'm the center of attention, if you dare!

Tell me more about that flower show,
My petals are blushing, don't you know?
I'm not just pretty, let's have some fun,
In the garden of jokes, I'm the only one!

So bring on the bees, I'll steal their buzz,
With every pollen joke, I'll leave you in fuzz!
An orchid's charm can't be contained,
In this floral world, I reign unchained!

On a sunny day, I'll make you grin,
With laughter sprouting from deep within!
So here's to my friends, the blooms so bright,
Together we laugh, what a joyful sight!

## **Lily Laughter Lines**

Floating gracefully on a pond,
I'm a lily, of this I'm fond.
With a wink from my waxy face,
I invite you all to join the race!

Why did the lily start to play?
Because boredom simply wouldn't stay!
With every ripple, I bring delight,
Comedy's enough to take flight!

In the company of reeds, I share a jest,
A lily like me? I'm simply the best!
So let's tiptoe into a flood of cheer,
Where giggles bloom from far and near!

As the sun dips low and skims the lake,
I'll make sure your sides start to ache!
With laughter weaving through the air,
This lily's here, let's spread the flair!

## Sunflower Shenanigans

Tall and bright, I wave hello,
With seeds of laughter in tow.
Why did the seed refuse to grow?
Because it found the light too slow!

Look at my face, it follows the sun,
In this garden, I'm here for fun!
Swinging and swaying, I catch some rays,
Creating sunshine through funny ways!

With petals wide, I spread good vibes,
No frowns allowed, just lively jibes!
When you pass by, don't forget to smile,
Sunflower joy can last a while!

So if you need a reason to laugh,
Just come to me, I'm fresh as a daff!
Join the party, don't miss the fun,
Together we shine, like moon and sun!

## Charmed by Chamomile

With a cup of tea, I bring good cheer,
My petals sway as you draw near.
I'm the calming kind that makes you sigh,
With every sip, let happiness fly!

Tell me your woes, I'll soak them in,
With charming rhymes, I'll start to spin.
I'm here for tea and tales of mirth,
In this garden, I'm known for worth!

So share a giggle, don't hold it back,
With chamomile blooms, we're on the right track!
Every sprout whispers sweet surprise,
In laughter's embrace, our spirits rise!

As twilight falls, let the stories flow,
With every sip, new laughter will glow!
Here's to the blooms that help us unwind,
In this fragrant world, joy is easy to find!

# The Floral Frolic

In gardens where the daisies dance,
The bees buzz about with a little prance.
They dip and dive with such delight,
In a flowery bash from morn till night.

A rose tried to rhyme, but fell on its face,
The tulips all giggled, oh what a place!
They whispered sweet jokes on sunny beams,
While sunflowers nodded, lost in their dreams.

The violets chuckled, 'We're not so shy!'
With blossoms so bright, they reached for the sky.
A daffodil joked, "Watch out for the breeze!"
"Or you might just end up down on your knees!"

With laughter and smiles in full blooming cheer,
These flowery folks spread joy far and near.
In the Floral Frolic, humor takes flight,
Where petals are playful, and the mood feels just right.

## **Budding Banter**

Two buds met in the morning light,
"Did you hear the joke? It's truly a sight!"
The first one giggled, "I'm all ears now,"
While bees buzzed around, taking a bow.

A sunflower chortled, "I'm bright and I know,
Why did the gardener give onions a show?"
The daffodils clapped, "The punchline was sweet!
Because they always make folks cry in defeat!"

The pansies were painted in colors so grand,
Playing cards with the wind, oh isn't it grand?
"Why did the rose send a letter of thanks?"
"Because it bloomed through the ranks!"

So here's to the buds with their laughter galore,
Creating a jolly that we can't ignore.
With snickers and chuckles, they dance on the way,
In the garden of joy, where they frolic and play.

## Poppy Playfulness

Poppies popped up, bright and bold,
Their playful antics never get old.
They tease the breeze with a flirty sway,
"Come join our game, it's a flower bouquet!"

In the meadow, a lily made a pun,
"I'm not just pretty, I'm practical fun!"
The daisies all giggled at this clever twist,
"Let's bloom together, there's nary a mist!"

A dandelion blew on a wishful thought,
"Should I plant more jokes or have I got caught?"
Amidst all the flora, the laughter is shared,
In the colorful chaos, no worries are bared.

So dance in the sunlight, let laughter ignite,
The poppy playfulness continues its flight.
In gardens of joy, where flowers are free,
With humor and smiles, we all share a spree.

## Daisy Drollery

Daisies gathered for a silly soirée,
Spinning tales that would brighten the day.
"Why did the garden get a good rest?"
"Because all of us flourished at our very best!"

With petals a-flutter and winks all around,
The daisies exchanged quips without making a sound.
"Did you hear about thyme? It's a herbal delight,
When cooking, it always gets things just right!"

The violets chimed in, "Oh, that's quite grand!"
"Why did the leaf go to the wonderland?"
A freckled young bloom said, "I'm not quite sure,
Because it wanted to explore and to cure!"

Embracing the laughter like sunshine on bloom,
In the daisy drollery, no thoughts of gloom.
So let's plant the seeds of joy in the field,
For fun and for laughter, this garden is healed.

## Garden Giggles

In a patch where daisies dance,
Silly bees wear polka pants.
They buzz around with flair so bright,
Throwing laughs from left to right.

The carrots wear their orange hues,
And gossip with the playful snooze.
With every sprout, a chuckle grows,
In this garden, humor flows.

Sunflowers tilt their heads for cheer,
They whisper jokes for all to hear.
While daisies crack a petal grin,
This joyous place, the fun begins.

So join the blooms, let laughter seed,
In this garden, joy takes lead.
For every flower's quirky tale,
Is just a laugh that cannot fail.

## Rosy Revelries

In the meadow, roses gleam,
Playing tricks, it's quite the dream.
One cracks jokes about its thorns,
While giggling in the gentle morns.

The tulips wear their colors bright,
Joking 'bout the sun's warm light.
They sway and twist in playful dance,
Drawing in the butterflies' glance.

A daffodil tells tales so tall,
Of adventures, fun for all.
With petals fluffed like fluffy clouds,
They spin their laughter, drawing crowds.

So join this space of floral cheer,
Where every bloom draws laughter near.
With rosy smiles that twitch and preen,
In this vibrant, playful scene.

## Stemmed Smiles

Beneath the leaves, the stems convene,
Telling stories of what they've seen.
With little giggles in the breeze,
They tease the birds up in the trees.

The sunbeams wink, the shadows play,
Creating jokes along the way.
While vines entwine in teasing holds,
Each laugh a tale that nature unfolds.

The thistle boasts with prickly pride,
While creeping clovers laugh and hide.
They sprout up tall, with smiles to share,
In this garden, joy fills the air.

So take a stroll, let laughter flow,
Among the stems, where spirits glow.
With every chuckle, roots dig deep,
In this playful patch, smiles leap.

## Foliage Fables

Leaves whisper secrets in the wind,
Of leafy legends, laughter pinned.
With every rustle, a story beams,
Where nature lives and humor dreams.

Oak trees joke of mighty height,
While ferns twirl in the soft twilight.
They twine their stories, weave them tight,
Creating smiles until the night.

A lilac chuckles, scent on air,
Crafting wishes without a care.
While mossy beds where dreamers lay,
Hold the laughter of the day.

So stroll through greens and see the fun,
In every shade beneath the sun.
For in this grove of leafy lore,
Laughter blooms forevermore.

## Botanical Buffoonery

In the garden of giggles, blooms so bright,
A daisy told a joke, what a sight!
The tulips laughed, their colors bold,
While the violets whispered secrets untold.

A sunflower winked with a radiant beam,
Said, "I've got seeds for your wildest dream!"
The marigolds danced, round and round,
In a festival of petals, joy abound.

The cacti quipped, with spines so stout,
"We're not just prickly, we're fun no doubt!"
And every blossom joined in the cheer,
In this lively garden, there's nothing to fear.

So come take a stroll, let laughter take flight,
In a world of blooms, everything feels right!

## Phlox Folly

At the edge of the blooms, in a patch of green,
Fritillary butterflies danced, twirling unseen.
The phloxes giggled, winking in the breeze,
"We're the life of the party, if you please!"

A bumblebee buzzed, with a laugh so sweet,
"I'm pollen my way through, can't miss this feat!"
The asters chimed in, with hats made of clay,
"Who wore it best? Let's debate all day!"

The garden was full of humorous flair,
With roses cracking puns, without a care.
"Why did the gardener get kicked from the set?
For sowing confusion, you can bet!"

Amidst the fun, the sun began to hide,
But laughter remained, like the bright blooms wide.

# Leafy Laughs

In the forest's embrace, where the leaves play,
The trees told tales of a windy day.
One oak with a grin said, "I'm quite the catch,
I hold all my secrets, just like a latch!"

The maples chimed in, a colorful crew,
"Let's flutter our leaves, just for a view!"
They tickled the breeze, with whispers of fun,
As the squirrel held court, under the sun.

A pine with a quirk, tall and quite proud,
"Do you know how to bark? I can say it loud!"
The willows just swayed, in rhythm and rhyme,
"Let's sway to the music, it's leaf-lovin' time!"

So they danced in the wind, their giggles a song,
In this leafy abode, where all feel they belong.

## **Rhododendron Riddles**

Underneath a canopy, blooms eye to eye,
Rhododendrons plotted, oh my, oh my!
"What's green and sings?" one asked with glee,
"Elvis Parsley! Can you not see?"

The azaleas chuckled, petals all a-flutter,
"Why did the flower blush? It saw the butter!"
With riddles exchanged, laughter took flight,
Their garden of humor a true delight.

With every poke and pun, the daisies joined in,
Why did the leaf cross the road? To win!
The blooms all agreed, humor should reign,
In a world of colors, a joyful refrain.

So next time you wander through gardens so bright,
Listen to whispers of humor and light.

## Rosy Riddles

Why did the rose blush so bright?
Because it saw the garden's delight.
It couldn't help but feel so bold,
In the sun, its beauty told.

What did the flower say to the bee?
"You're buzzing by a beauty, see?"
With a wink and a little sway,
The petals danced and laughed all day.

Why do daisies never get lost?
Their paths are clear, it's worth the cost.
With sunny faces shining wide,
They'll guide you, friend, with petal pride.

What joke did violets share at night?
"Let's bloom and giggle until it's light!"
In each petal, laughter tucked,
The garden's joy will never be plucked.

## Cheerful Cacti

Why did the cactus smile so wide?
It loved the sun, its wild ride.
With spines that poke but humor true,
It always welcomes friends like you.

What did the prickly pear declare?
"I'm sweet inside, if you dare!"
With a grin, it took a chance,
Inviting all for a fun dance.

Why don't cacti ever feel blue?
Their jokes are sharp, and laughter too.
In the desert, with friends so bright,
They share the joy both day and night.

What's a cactus' favorite game?
Hide and seek with sunshine's flame.
With clever tricks and playful cheer,
They giggle loud, not showing fear.

## Amusing Azaleas

Why do azaleas love to tease?
They know how to sway with the breeze.
In colors bright, they wink and say,
"Bloom with laughter, let's play today!"

What did one azalea say to its mate?
"You're such a bud, let's celebrate!"
With petals soft and jokes to share,
They spiral around, without a care.

Why do azaleas dance in the rain?
To wash away all hints of pain.
With drops like pearls, they twist and twirl,
Their charm and giggles make hearts whirl.

How do azaleas say goodbye?
They toss their petals, oh so sly.
With laughter ringing in the air,
Their beauty lingers, everywhere.

## **Giggles in the Greenhouse**

In the greenhouse, laughter streams,
Where leaves awaken from their dreams.
Each plant tells a joke or two,
In leafy whispers, just for you.

What's a plant's favorite time of year?
When blooms arrive, the joy is clear!
With colors bright and scents so sweet,
They throw a bash, it's quite the treat!

Why do veggies love a chat?
They share their woes, they share their sprat.
In rows they stand, all side by side,
With giggles blooming, hearts full of pride.

What happened to the shy little fern?
It finally found its voice to learn.
With every curl, it spun a tale,
In giggles soft, the laughter sails.

## Nature's Nonsense

In the garden of giggles, blooms laugh so loud,
Daisies tell jokes, while the roses are proud.
Sunflowers wink, with their golden surprise,
While the shy violets hide, avoiding the eyes.

Butterflies dance with a fluttering cheer,
Tickling the daisies, oh what a queer!
A potato on vacation, what a sight,
It rolled down the hill, lost in delight!

Bumblebees buzzing a silly sweet tune,
They'll steal all your honey, oh what a swoon!
Tulips are teasing, they sway to and fro,
While daisies gossip, putting on quite a show.

In Nature's strange circus, the fun doesn't cease,
Laughter erupts, oh what a release!
Every bloom adds a little zing,
Together they make the wildflowers sing!

## The Pansy Parade

Pansies prance in a colorful row,
Waving their arms, putting on a show.
A sunflower struts, with a big, goofy grin,
While ladybugs giggle, spinning in spin.

Petunias perform a tap on the green,
With glances so sly, they know what they mean.
Marigolds march in the soft morning light,
As the lazy daisies nap, avoiding the fright.

A giggly garden, with laughter galore,
The fragrance of fun, who could ask for more?
With pollen-packed puns and a bee's little sting,
The flowers, they flirt, and the butterflies sing!

Come join the parade, there's joy everywhere,
Where blossoms are silly, and garden gnomes stare.
A flourish of colors and smiles to encase,
In the Pansy Parade, find joy in each space!

## Witty Wildflowers

Wildflowers whisper with humor so light,
Tickled by breezes, they tease in delight.
A daffodil jokes, with a flair in its pose,
While a poppy snickers, hiding its nose.

In a patch of bright colors, the chuckles run free,
Forget-me-nots giggle, with glee exponentially.
A dandelion sneezes, pollen takes flight,
A riot of laughter, oh what a sight!

Chicory chimes in, with a wink and a nod,
A sage brush will share, "Was it me or the fog?"
Rosemary's scent adds to the zest,
Together they concoct the garden's best jest.

Every flower stands up, plays a quirky part,
In this witty wonderland, joy's an art.
So stop for a moment, and just take a look,
At the cleverness written in Nature's own book!

## The Hilarity of Hibiscus

Oh hibiscus, you jest, with petals so bright,
You make garden parties a marvelous sight.
Winking at pollinators, oh what a flair,
While sipping sweet nectar, they don't have a care.

"Why did the flower blush?" giggles arise,
"Because it saw the bumblebee working in guise!"
With laughter that echoes in tropical air,
The hibiscus brings joy, that's fabulously rare.

Cactus cracks jokes, with prickly insight,
While hiding their laughs, 'til day turns to night.
"Don't leaf me hanging," a petunia will pout,
As acorns chuckle, with giggles throughout.

The humor is flowing, like wisteria vine,
In the hilarious garden, the sun starts to shine.
With each bright bloom ready to share their delight,
The hibiscus brings laughter, so joyous and bright!

## Sprightly Spiraeas

In gardens where the spiraeas play,
They giggle in the sun all day.
Their leaves all dance in breezy cheer,
Whispering jokes for all to hear.

With every bloom, a joke takes flight,
They tickle petals, oh what a sight!
A bee rolls by with a buzzing grin,
'You think you're funny? Just wait, I'll win!'

When daisies mock with playful jive,
The spiraeas leap and start to thrive.
Each color splashes like laughter's sound,
Creating joy that knows no bound.

So raise your glass, toast to this bloom,
The sprightly spiraeas chase the gloom.
With every cherry red they boast,
They're the funniest flowers, let's raise a toast!

## Frolicking Foliage

The leaves are swirling in a merry spin,
With laughter twinkling from within.
Each branch with tales of funny sights,
Like squirrels in socks on balmy nights.

Lush greens frolic, whispering cheer,
Tickling the trunks, "Hey, over here!"
A sunbeam giggles through every hue,
'Why do the trees need shoes, who knew?'

As autumn paints with a chuckle bright,
The foliage puts on a comical sight.
Each leaf a clown, a wink, a smile,
Their funny dance, a leafy style.

So join the frolic, don't stand alone,
In this leafy laughter, we've all grown.
With nature's humor, let's spread the cheer,
Frolicking foliage, forever near!

## Blooming Buffoons

In the patch of colors, buffoons arise,
Blooming flowers with giggling sighs.
With petals bright and faces fair,
They tell stories of who sat where.

A sunflower nods with a knowing wink,
'Why did the rose stop to think?'
The tulip chimes in with a hearty laugh,
'Why did you ask, you're not a staff!'

Every bloom knows a pun to share,
Tickling bees drifting in the air.
A daisy lays down a water joke,
'Why's it so wet? Because I spoke!'

So gather 'round this garden play,
The blooming buffoons are here to stay.
With petals laughing, let's brighten the day,
Join the fun, don't shy away!

## Sassy Sassafras

The sassafras tree struts with flair,
Chatting with breezes, it doesn't care.
With leaves that tease and bark that jokes,
It boasts to the sun, 'I'm one of the folks!'

'Why don't trees like to play hide and seek?
Because they can't see, they're too sleek!'
The sassafras chuckles, twisting around,
With humor stitched deeply into the ground.

Breeze whispers secrets of who brings fun,
While acorns giggle in their tiny run.
Each branching laughter, a tree-topped cheer,
The sassafras shines with no hint of fear.

So join the sass, let's celebrate trees,
With laughter and joy carried on the breeze.
In this sassy realm, we'll dance and tease,
Creating memories among the leaves!

## Orchid Oddities

Orchids striking, quite the sight,
Wearing polka dots that are bright.
They giggle when the raindrops fall,
Whispering jokes to one and all.

Dancing leaves in the warm sunlight,
Doing the cha-cha, what a delight!
With roots that tickle under the ground,
Their laughter echoes all around.

Some say they're just a little vain,
For in mirrors, they love to gaze.
Having hairdos that twist and twirl,
Who knew plants could be such a whirl?

Isn't it funny, their silly grace?
In the parade of the garden space.
They whisper secrets, share a grin,
In the world of blooms, let the fun begin!

## Botanical Buffoonery

In the garden, laughter prevails,
With dandelions that tell tall tales.
Sunflowers giggle, their heads held high,
While clover skips by, waving goodbye.

The tulips throw a wild flower bash,
With petals twirling in a colorful clash.
Each color a punchline, sharp and bright,
Holding their breath, they bloom with delight.

Lilies wear sunglasses, cool as can be,
Joking about bees and their busy spree.
With roots in jest and stems of cheer,
These botanical jesters bring good vibes near.

So let's celebrate the plant parade,
Where even the weeds have a grand charade!
In a garden of giggles, let's plant our fun,
As laughter sprouts 'neath the warming sun.

**Petals and Punchlines**

Roses in blush whisper wisecracks,
While daisies plot their next big hacks.
Violets chuckle, their laughter sweet,
With puns hidden among their leafy seat.

Chrysanthemums giggle, wearing crowns,
Joking about how they won't frown.
They throw shade while catching some rays,
In the sun's spotlight, they love to amaze.

Morning glory climbs with a twinkling wink,
Saying, 'Life's short, don't forget to think!'
While marigolds joke about turning gold,
Planting funny tales that never get old.

With roots in humor and leaves in jest,
Each bloom creates a playful quest.
In this garden of laughs, we'll always find,
A punchline or two to brighten the mind!

## Waggish Wartworts

Wartworts wear their quirky hats,
With polka-dotted skirts that chat.
They roll in the mud, oh what a scene,
Making mud pies, so sprightly and keen.

With friends like fungi, they dance all day,
Throwing wild parties in a cheeky way.
Their laughter bubbles from the ground,
In the soil, their humor knows no bounds.

Even crickets join in their fun show,
With rhythms that make the garden grow.
Bees buzz around, adding to the cheer,
As wartworts chuckle, their antics clear.

So here's to the plants, so waggish and spry,
In their green world, laughter will never die!
With quirks and giggles, they charm the sun,
In this realm of blooms, there's always fun!

www.ingramcontent.com/pod-product-compliance
Lightning Source LLC
Chambersburg PA
CBHW051639160426
43209CB00004B/709